It Can Be Romantic

Recipes and Ideas From
International Settings for Romantic Evenings
at Home

Bill Deegan   **Rebecca Deegan**

Lulu
www.Lulu.com

ISBN: 978-0-615-24845-5

About the Authors

Bill and Rebecca Deegan have been experimenting with food, travel, and international locations for over 30 years. They have traveled extensively and tried a good deal of the world's cuisine. Their trips have produced ideas for romantic settings and menus created from personal experiences abroad in many countries throughout the world and from cooking at home.

This book is the first in a series of five to be organized around romantic international settings and gourmet food.

Contents

Introduction

A Recipe for Romance

- The world can be a difficult place. Once per month treat yourself to a wonderful fantasy escape. The evenings suggested are for romance and gourmet dining. The recipes for two are international but easy to prepare. Some dishes can be made ahead. The idea is to have the fun and creativity of making something together, but with time for a romantic and interesting evening.

- Anticipation is a large part of the fun. Once a month:

    - Pick a theme; for example, choose an evening in Paris.
    - Build up to it; read books and magazines about the theme country; rent movies and travel videos for insights.
    - Buy music that is from the theme country.
    - Buy something special to wear to add to the spirit of the evening.
    - Decorate your table and dining area to celebrate the country you are experiencing.

- Create a romantic atmosphere.

- Set a beautiful table with

    - Candlelight   - Flowers   - China/Silver
    - Linen   - Lighting   - Music

Take a month to build to each evening. Then enjoy and escape to a series of wonderful fantasy evenings. Let your creativity take over and your inhibitions go. We think you will agree: **It Can Be Romantic!**

Paris

April in Paris: An Evening on the Left Bank

April in Paris: An Evening on the Left Bank

The Place - Paris: City of Light and Romance!

Imagine you have had a day of shopping on the Rue du Faubourg St.-Honore. In the late afternoon you take a tour of the old opera house with its grand staircase. At dusk you leave on a boat ride down the Seine River like Cary Grant and Audrey Hepburn in the movie <u>Charade</u>. Later you wander along the narrow streets just off the Boulevard St. Michel near the Sorbonne and find a wonderful French restaurant. Inside there is candlelight, lace curtains, soft music, and wonderful ambiance.

Create your own version of Paris elegance. Build up to the evening all month long.

- **Buy some magazines and books about Parisian life.**

- **Wander through some stores than carry French goods.**

- **Rent a movie or two set in Paris or a travel video on Paris**

- **Purchase some French music such as Edith Piaf or Charles Aznevoir to help set the mood for the evening.**

- **Purchase something French to wear.**

- **Decorate your table with a French theme.**

Add your own creative flair and escape to a **Romantic Evening in Paris!**

The Menu

- Pernod over Ice

- Stuffed Mushroom Caps

- Chicken Veronique

- French Green Beans

- Rice St. Michele

- Grand Marnier Crepes

Wine

Chardonnay – Pouilly Fuisse

Start your evening by sampling a glass of Pernod over ice with a splash of water… a favorite café drink.

Stuffed Mushrooms

Ingredients

8 medium-small mushrooms
1 tablespoon butter
1 tablespoon minced shallots or onion
¼ teaspoon Worcestershire sauce
1/3 cup seasoned breadcrumbs
¼ cup shredded sharp cheese
salt and pepper to taste
2 tablespoons water

Directions

Preheat oven to 350 degrees F.
Wash mushrooms and drain.
Pull stems from mushrooms and finely chop stems.
Melt butter in a small skillet.
Add shallots and chopped mushrooms. Saute until tender.
Stir in Worcestershire sauce, salt, pepper, and breadcrumbs.
Salt insides of mushroom caps and fill with sauté mixture.
Top with shredded cheese.
Put two tablespoons water in a shallow dish, arrange mushrooms in dish, and bake about 20 minutes.

- (This dish can be made ahead and refrigerated for 24 hours.)

Prep Time: 20 minutes   Serves: Two

Chicken Veronique

Ingredients

2 tablespoons sweet butter
2 half boneless, skinless chicken breasts
2 tablespoons dry white wine
½ teaspoon tarragon
¼ teaspoon salt
½ cup whipping cream
½ cup seedless green grapes

Directions

Heat butter in an eight-inch skillet over medium heat.
Rinse chicken breasts and dry on paper towels.
Saute chicken breasts until tender and golden on both sides.
Add wine, tarragon, and salt.
Cover and simmer about two to five minutes.
Place chicken breasts on a plate and cover to keep warm.
Quickly boil pan juices until like a syrup.
Add whipping cream.
Boil until slightly thickened.
Lower heat and stir grapes into cream mixture.
Put chicken back in pan for 30 seconds to warm.
Arrange chicken on plates and spoon sauce and grapes on top.

Prep/Cook Time: 20 minutes   Serves: Two

French Green Beans

Ingredients

½ pound fresh green beans
¾ cup water for steaming
1 teaspoon finely chopped scallions
Salt and freshly ground black pepper to taste

Directions

Wash the beans, trim the ends, and cut them into 1 ½ -inch pieces. Bring the water to boil in a small saucepan. Place the beans into steamer basket and cover pan. Steam for 15 minutes. Drain, add the scallions, and season with salt and pepper.

Prep Time: 10 minutes

Serves: Two

Rice St. Michele

Ingredients

2 tablespoons butter
½ cup uncooked long grain rice
1 tablespoon slivered almonds
1 cup chicken stock

Directions

Heat butter in a small pan over medium heat.
Add rice.
Saute until rice is golden.
Add chicken stock.
Bring to a boil. Reduce heat to slow simmer for about 15 minutes.
Remove from heat. Let stand covered for five minutes.
Salt and pepper to taste.
Add slivered almonds.

To delay evening, reduce heat to low and add two tablespoons water. Reheat when needed.

Prep/Cook Time: 15 minutes

Serves: Two

Grand Marnier Crepes

Ingredients

½ cup water
½ cup whole milk
2 large eggs.
1 cup all-purpose plain flour
2 teaspoons sugar
1 teaspoon vanilla
For sauce - 4 tablespoons sugar
4 tablespoons unsalted butter
1 orange for grated zest
½ cup Grand Marnier
French vanilla ice cream

Directions

To prepare crepes, combine water, milk, eggs, flour, sugar, and vanilla. Blend until very smooth in blender. Cover and refrigerate for 1 hour. Grease a nonstick 9-inch crepe or frying pan lightly and place over medium heat. Scoop two – three tablespoons of batter into the pan and swirl the pan to cover the bottom evenly with batter. Cook about one minute until the crepe begins to bubble and brown a little. Place on waxed paper. Use remaining batter to prepare additional crepes. Stack crepes between waxed paper sheets.

Melt butter with sugar and grated orange zest in nonstick frying pan. Heat until the mixture is foamy, about one to two minutes. Remove from heat and add Grand Marnier to the pan. Stir to combine. Remove crepes from waxed paper and fold each crepe in half

Return the Grand Marnier mixture in the pan to heat for about one minute. Place crepes in the pan and heat for about one minute on each side, turning them with tongs to coat on each side evenly. Place crepes on each warmed dessert plate and spoon sauce on servings. Add a scoop of French vanilla ice cream to each serving.

Prep Time: 20 minutes   Serves: 2

New York

**The Way You Look Tonight:
New York – 65 Stories Up**

The Way You Look Tonight:
New York – 65 Stories Up

The Place – New York: City of Money, Fashion, and Power

Imagine that you spent the morning visiting your investment advisor on Wall Street and the afternoon shopping on Fifth Avenue. In the late afternoon you visit the Museum of Modern Art to see the new display.   In the evening you take an elevator 65 floors up to an intimate, dimly lighted restaurant. You are shown to a table with a spectacular view of the city below. The lights of Manhattan remind you of the power, energy, and creativity of New York. The city pulsates below as you enjoy the view over cocktails.

Create your own New York penthouse restaurant for an evening:

- **Buy magazines that feature New York and the Sunday "New York Times".**

- **Purchase some New York kind of music – Frank Sinatra, Michael Finestein, Andrea Marcovecci.**

- **Rent a Movie featuring New York – "You've Got Mail", "Wall Street", or a travel video on New York.**

- **Dress for the evening.**

Make it a night of "at home elegance" to celebrate **New York – 65 Stories Up!!**

The Menu

- Vodka Martinis

- Avocado and Crabmeat

- Madison Avenue Salad

- Lamb 5th Avenue

- Soho Buttered Asparagus

- Potatoes Au Gratin

- Lemon Mousse

Wine

Merlot

Begin your evening with a Vodka Martini and Hors D'oeuvres.

Vodka Martini

Ingredients

6 oz. Vodka
1 thin slice lemon peel
2 stuffed olives
ice

Directions

Place 6 oz. Of Vodka, one thin slice of lemon peel into Martini tumbler filled with ice to ¾ full. Shake 65 times. Pour into two martini glasses. Garnish with olives to taste.
Enjoy!

Prep Time: 10 minutes   Serves: 2

This Hors D'oeuvre may be prepared ahead of time to allow flavors of the ingredients to blend.

Avocado and Crabmeat

Ingredients

1 firm avocado
1 cup fresh crabmeat
½ cup chopped celery
½ cup chopped cucumber
½ cup light mayonnaise
salt and freshly ground pepper

Directions

Combine crabmeat, celery, cucumber, dash of salt/pepper, and mayonnaise in a small mixing bowl. Blend well.
Cut avocado in half lengthwise. Remove the pit from center. Scoop prepared crabmeat into each half of avocado. Refrigerate until serving time.

Prep Time: 15 minutes   Serves: 2

This salad may be prepared ahead of time and refrigerated for convenience.

Madison Avenue Salad

Ingredients

Fresh spinach for two
¼ cup olive oil
1 small red onion
1 hard-boiled egg
2 tablespoons wine vinegar
¼ teaspoon salt
2 tablespoons grated Parmesan cheese
salt and pepper

Directions

Wash spinach, dry, remove stems, and tear into small pieces.
Cover spinach with damp paper towel and refrigerate to crisp.
Chop hard-boiled egg into bite size slices.
Slice onion into small rings.
Blend vinegar, oil, salt and pepper in a small bowl.
Refrigerate until ready to serve.

Add dressing, egg slices, onion rings, and sprinkle with Parmesan cheese on top. Enjoy!!

Prep Time: 20 minutes

Serves: 2

Lamb Fifth Avenue

Ingredients

4 lean lamb loin chops (1¼ in. thick)
3 tablespoons melted butter
1 tablespoon olive oil
½ teaspoon rosemary (finely crushed)
1 tablespoon lemon juice
1 clove garlic minced
1 tablespoon finely chopped parsley

Directions

In a small bowl stir together melted butter, garlic, olive oil, parsley, crushed rosemary, and lemon juice until well blended.
Cover and refrigerate until needed.

Broiling Directions

For lamb loin chops 1 ¼ inches thick, place on unheated rack of broiler pan 5-6 inches from heat.

For rare: Broil approximately 8-10 minutes (4-5 min. per side).
For medium: Broil approximately 10-12 minutes (5-6 min. per side).

Remove butter mixture from refrigerator and heat thoroughly.
Pour the hot mixture over lamb loin chops, and serve immediately.

Prep Time: 20 minutes   Serves: 2

Soho Buttered Asparagus

Ingredients

10 pieces fresh asparagus
¼ cup melted butter
2 tablespoons lemon juice
2 tablespoons snipped parsley
½ teaspoon salt
Dash pepper

Directions

Scrub asparagus gently, clipping tough ends.
Cook whole spears covered in small amount of boiling water for 10-15 minutes.

Melt ¼ cup butter. Add two tablespoons lemon juice, two tablespoons snipped parsley, ½
teaspoon salt, and dash pepper.
Heat and serve over asparagus.

Prep Time: 25 minutes   Serves: 2

Potatoes Au Gratin

Ingredients

¼ cup butter, melted
¼ cup sifted all-purpose flour
1 teaspoon salt
¼ teaspoon pepper
2 cups milk
1 cup freshly grated sharp cheese
3 cups cooked, hot-diced potatoes
(4 medium potatoes)
2 tablespoons butter, melted
½ cup dry bread crumbs
1 tablespoon parsley
1 tablespoon paprika

Directions

White Sauce
Melt butter in saucepan over low heat.
Blend in flour, salt, and pepper. Add milk gradually.
Quickly cook mixture, stirring constantly, until thick, bubbling, and smooth. Remove from heat.
Blend white sauce mixture and cheese; combine with hot diced potatoes. Pour into a 1-quart casserole. Toss crumbs with melted butter and parsley. Sprinkle on top of potatoes.
Sprinkle with paprika.
Bake at 350 degrees F. for 20-25 minutes or until browned.

Prep Time: 30 minutes   Serves: 2

Lemon Mousse

Ingredients

12 graham crackers
1 small can (2/3 cup) of evaporated milk
1 cup of sugar
1 tablespoon grated lemon peel
the juice of 2 lemons

Directions

Chill milk in freezer until almost frozen. Put milk in a cold bowl and whip. Add to the whip the lemon peel and slowly add juice of lemons. Beat continuously. Cover bottom of pyrex oblong dish 8 in. x 8 in. with crushed graham crackers. Set aside ¼ cup of crushed crackers. Pour mixture over graham crackers. Spread evenly to sides.
Sprinkle ¼ cup of remaining crushed graham crackers over top surface.
Freeze for at least two hours before serving.

Prep Time: 20 minutes

Ireland

An Irish Castle Candlelight Dinner

An Irish Castle Candlelight Dinner

The Place – Ireland: Land of Green Hills, Rugged Coasts, Leprechauns, Warm Pubs, And Friendly People

Imagine you have spent a day exploring a small Irish village near Galway. A walk through rugged countryside passing charming cottages with thatched roofs brings you back to the large stone castle where you are staying. Towering walls of stone, wonderfully polished wood and a roaring fire in the fireplace greet you as you enter.

Create your own evening in an Irish castle. Build up to it by purchasing some magazines and newspapers from Ireland.

- **Read a travel book about Irish castles and countryside.**

- **Rent a travel video on Ireland or movies such as <u>Ryan's Daughter</u> or <u>The Quiet Man</u>.**

- **Read about Irish history.**

- **Purchase some Irish music-from the Irish Rovers to U-2. .**

- **Visit an Irish shop and purchase something.**

Plan your evening around St. Patrick's Day to further capture some of the ambiance of the evening. **Enjoy a romantic Irish Castle Candlelight Dinner!!**

The Menu

- Eileen's Irish Soda Bread

- Salmon Steaks with Mushroom Stuffing

- Killarney Potatoes

- Herbed Carrots

- Wexford Pudding

- Irish Coffee

Wine

Pinot Noir

or

Chardonnay

Eileen's Irish Soda Bread

Ingredients

4 cups sifted flour
1 ½ teaspoon soda
1 teaspoon salt
2 tablespoons caraway seeds
¾ cups sugar
1 cup raisins
2 tablespoons butter (melted after measuring)
2 eggs beaten lightly
1 ½ cup buttermilk

Directions

Sift flour, soda, and salt into bowl.
Add caraway seeds, sugar, and raisins; mix.
Mix butter, beaten eggs, and buttermilk.
Stir into flour mixture.
After forming into a round loaf, place in a round greased pan.
With a knife cut a cross on top of loaf.
Bake at 350 degrees F. for one and one-fourth hours.

Let cool for few minutes. Brush with melted butter.
Cool completely and wrap in aluminum foil.

Prep Time: 20 min.

Serves: 2

Salmon Fillets With Mushroom Stuffing

Ingredients

3 salmon fillets (¾ in. of equal size)
¼ teaspoon salt
¼ cup butter
¼ cup finely chopped onion
½ cup light cream
1 ½ cup soft bread crumbs
1 cup sliced fresh mushrooms
1 tablespoon chopped parsley
½ tablespoon lemon juice
¼ teaspoon salt
¼ teaspoon pepper

Directions

Sprinkle salmon fillets with salt.
Melt butter in skillet; sauté onion in butter until tender.
Combine onion with crumbs, mushrooms, parsley, lemon juice, salt and pepper to make stuffing..
Cut salmon fillets in half, lengthwise.
Place three halves of salmon fillets in a buttered baking dish.
Spoon 1/3 of the mushroom stuffing on top of each steak.
Cover with remaining halves of steaks.
Pour cream over tops.
Bake at 350 degrees F., basting occasionally, for 30-40 minutes, until salmon flakes.

Prep Time: 20 min.   Cook Time: 30-40 min.   Serves: 2

Killarney Potatoes

Ingredients

2 large baking potatoes
¾ cup cream-style cottage cheese with chives
2 teaspoons shredded cheddar cheese
1 teaspoon chopped pimiento
milk as needed

Directions

Scrub potatoes; prick skins.
Bake in a 425 degrees F. oven about 1 hour and 10 minutes.
Cut potatoes in half lengthwise.
Scoop out insides leaving ¼ inch shells.
Mash potatoes.
Beat in cottage cheese, pimiento, and ¼ teaspoon salt.
If necessary, beat in enough milk to make fluffy.
Spoon into potato shells.
Sprinkle cheddar cheese on tops.
Bake, covered, in a 350 degrees oven for 25 minutes
or until heated through.

Prep Time: 15 min.   Serves: 2

Herbed Carrots

Ingredients

10 slender carrots
3 tablespoons butter
¼ cup minced parsley
salt and pepper

Directions

In a wide frying pan, lay carrots flat.
Add water to cover and bring to boil.
Reduce heat to simmer.
Cook until carrots are tender (15-20 min.).
Drain.
Add butter. Cook over medium heat, shaking pan until carrots are lightly browned on all sides. Mix in parsley.
Salt and pepper to taste.

Prep/Cook Time: 25 min.   Serves: 2

Wexford Pudding

Ingredients

1 loaf white bread, cubed
4 tablespoons butter, melted
3 cups milk
4 eggs, beaten
½ cup sugar
1 tablespoon vanilla
1 teaspoon cinnamon
½ teaspoon nutmeg

Rum Sauce:

½ cup rum
½ cup milk
2 cups vanilla ice cream

Directions

Preheat oven to 375 degrees F.
Place bread cubes in a greased 9 inch baking dish and drizzle with melted butter. In a saucepan, scald milk and stir in beaten eggs, sugar, vanilla, and spices. Pour over the bread and mix to moisten.
Bake 30 minutes.

For Rum Sauce, blend ingredients in a blender until creamy and smooth.
Serve with the warm bread pudding.

Prep/Cook Time: 55 min.

Irish Coffee

Ingredients

2 cups coffee
2 oz. Irish Whisky
1 cup whipped cream

Directions

Stir into warm coffee filled cups 1 oz. each of the Irish Whisky.
Top with a mound of whipped cream.
Enjoy together for a delightful evening!!

Prep Time: 5 min.   Serves: 2

Shanghai

An Evening in Shanghai

An Evening In Shanghai

The Place-Shanghai: Bustling Business Capital Combining a Rich Mixture of Old Traditions and Modern Systems

Imagine a day exploring the cultural and historical riches of Shanghai. You spend part of the day exploring the Bund (Shanghai's waterfront boulevard) on the bank of the Huangpu River. You later visit the old French Concession area with its tree-lined streets and cozy cafes along with the old city area of stone gate houses, temples and markets.

In the evening you wander down the Nanjing Road. The lights of night illuminate a wonderland of shops and restaurants. You find a beautiful restaurant complete with hanging colorful lanterns and candles.

Create your own evening in Shanghai.

- **Read a history of China.**

- **Rent movies and travel videos about China and its culture.**

- **Find some music in the Chinese tradition.**

- **Look for magazines featuring stories and fashions from China.**

- **Purchase something Chinese to wear and a couple of decorations or hanging lanterns.**

- **Buy a wok, start the music, light the candles, and travel to China for An Evening in Shanghai!!**

The Menu

- Sesame Shrimp Toast

- Scallops with Ginger

- Shanghai Vegetable Medley

- Steamed Rice

- Lychee Paradise Mound

- Fortune Cookies (Purchased)

Wine

Sauvignon Blanc

Or

Chardonnay

Sesame Shrimp Toast

Ingredients

6 large freshly boiled shrimp
1 tablespoon lemon juice
1 cup finely chopped celery
¼ cup mayonnaise
½ cup sesame seeds
Salt and pepper
For pieces of toast-3 slices of white bread

Directions

Chop shrimp in bits and pieces.
Sprinkle with lemon juice.
Add celery and mayonnaise.
Toss lightly; season with salt and pepper. Chill.
Spread on toast, and sprinkle tops with sesame seeds.

For toast-
Toast the white bread until lightly browned. Remove the crusts with a serrated knife.
Cut through each slice horizontally.
Then cut each slice into triangles.
Place the triangles on a cookie sheet, lighter side up, and broil until lightly browned.
Remove from the oven and allow the toast to cool.
Note: Watch the broiler closely, or the toast will burn within seconds.

Scallops with Ginger

Ingredients

6 fresh large scallops
¼ teaspoon ground white pepper
2 tablespoons soy sauce
2 tablespoons dry sherry
2 spring onions, white part only cut into long shreds
2 tablespoons oil
ginger, 2 inches in length, peeled and shredded

Directions

Sprinkle scallops with the pepper.
Combine soy and sherry in a small bowl.
Heat the oil in large, heavy-based pan until hot.
Add scallops face down and cook for 30 seconds to sear.
Turn face up and arrange on a heatproof dish.
Sprinkle scallops with sherry-soy mixture and scatter a few shreds of ginger and spring onion over.
Fill a wok or wide frying pan one-third with water; bring to a boil. Place a steamer in the wok; place scallops on it. Cover wok tightly and steam for one minute.
Check for doneness. Remove and keep warm.
It is best to prepare this dish just before serving.

Prep/Cook Time: 15 min.   Serves: 2

Shanghai Vegetable Medley

Ingredients

1 (8oz.)can water chestnuts, drained
1 (8oz.) can bamboo shoots, drained
20 snow peas (ends snapped off)
½ red bell pepper cut into 1 inch pieces
2 tablespoons salad oil
2 tablespoons soy sauce
1small garlic clove (minced)
Salt and pepper

Directions

Heat a wok or wide frying pan over high heat.
When pan is hot, add oil.
When oil begins to heat, add garlic.
Stir once around pan.
Add vegetables and stir-fry for 1 minute to coat with oil.
Add salt, soy sauce, cover, and cook until vegetables are crisp-tender (about 2 minutes).

Steamed Rice

Ingredients

1 cup long grain rice
2 cups water

Directions

Combine water, salt and rice in a small saucepan. Cover tightly and bring to boil. Reduce heat to a very low simmer. Cook about 15 minutes until all water is absorbed. Do not lift lid during cooking. Fluff with a fork before serving.

Lychee Paradise Mound

Ingredients

¼ cup sugar
1 tablespoon cornstarch
1 can lychees
2 teaspoons butter
2 tablespoons lime juice

Four scoops of vanilla ice cream

Directions

Mix together sugar and cornstarch in a pan.
Drain syrup from lychees (1 can).
Blend into cornstarch mixture. Add butter and cook, stirring, until sauce bubbles and thickens (about 2 minutes.). Remove from heat and stir in lychees and juice from lime.
Serve warm or at room temperature spooned over ice cream.

Serve with purchased Fortune Cookies.

Prep/Cook Time: 15 min.   Serves: 2

England

A Weekend in the English Countryside

A Weekend in the English Countryside

The Place- England: Land of Kings and Queens, Shakespeare, Sherlock Holmes, and Dickens!

From cosmopolitan London to the hills and villages of the Lake District to the rugged coastline, England is a land of wonderful sights and warm people. Imagine you are staying in an old Tudor house in the English countryside. It is a cold, windy evening. Down the road is a very old country inn full of cheerful people , soft lighting, delicious food, and a warm fireplace. You enter the inn and are seated at a corner table with a view of the fireplace.

Create your own English country inn on a cold autumn evening.

- **Buy the Sunday "London Times".**

- **Rent movies such as <u>The Hound of the Baskervilles</u> or <u>Shakespeare In Love.</u>**

- **Rent a travel video on England.**

- **Read Dickens, Shakespeare, or the great English romantic poets (perhaps Shelley and Keats) or other English writers.**

- **Enjoy the music of English artists—from Noel Coward to the Beatles to the London Symphony!**

Build a roaring fire, light lots of candles, dim the lights, and travel to **A Weekend in the English Countryside.**

The Menu

- Shrimp Cocktail in Surrey Sauce

- Kensington Roast Beef and Yorkshire Pudding

- Fresh Brussels Sprouts with Chestnuts and Thyme

- Kent Cranberry Chill

- Blackberry Tarts with Devonshire Sauce

Wine

Cabernet Sauvignon

Shrimp Cocktail in Surry Sauce

Ingredients

8 boiled large shrimp

Surrey Sauce
2 teaspoons grated onion
1 tablespoon lemon juice
¼ cup chili sauce
1 teaspoon prepared horseradish
½ teaspoon Worcestershire sauce
Dash Tabasco sauce
Salt to taste
Freshly ground black pepper to taste

Directions

Surrey Sauce
Combine all ingredients in a small bowl.
Refrigerate for two hours.
Arrange shrimp on a serving plate with surrey sauce in a small bowl in the center for dipping.

Kensington Roast Beef

Ingredients

2 pound prime beef rib roast – boned and tied
¾ teaspoon coarse Kosher salt
½ teaspoon freshly ground black pepper
¼ cup fresh garlic minced
¾ tablespoon chopped fresh rosemary
½ cup olive oil

Directions

Combine salt, spices, garlic in small mixing bowl.
Place roast, fat side up, on a rack in an open roasting pan.
Brush roast with olive oil, and rub or press salt, pepper, garlic, and spices onto the meat's surface.
Preheat the oven to 325 degrees.
Insert meat thermometer so bulb reaches center of the thickest part of roast, making sure that bulb does not rest in fat or on bone. (Do not add water or cover.)
Optional: Cut several small slits in meat and insert minced fresh garlic.
Roast in 325 degrees oven to the desired degree of doneness. Meat thermometer will register 140 degree for rare; 160 degree for medium; 170 degree for well done.
Allow 23 to 25 minutes per pound for cooking roast to rare, 27 to 30 minutes for medium, and 32 to 35 minutes for well done. (Roasts are easier to carve if allowed to stand 20 to 30 minutes after they are removed from oven.)
Since roasts continue to cook during this standing period, it is best to remove the roast when the thermometer registers about 5 degrees below the temperature desired.

Yorkshire Pudding

Ingredients

1 cup sifted all-purpose flour
¾ teaspoon salt
2 eggs
1 cup of milk
¼ cup drippings from roast beef

Directions

Heat a small muffin tin in 400 degrees oven for 5 minutes.
Sift together flour and salt. Beat eggs. Add milk; slowly beat in dry ingredients. Spoon 1-2 teaspoons of beef drippings from roasting pan into each of the 6 hot muffin cups. Divide batter equally, approximately 3 ½ tablespoons in each cup.
Bake in oven preheated to 400 degrees F. for 30 minutes or until puddings are golden brown.
Serve with roast.
Heat remaining juices in roasting pan and serve over puddings, if desired.

Prep/Cook Time: 45 minutes

Serves: 2

Kent Cranberry Chill

Ingredients

1 cup of sugar
1½ cups of water
2 cups fresh cranberries

Directions

Combine sugar and water in saucepan; stir to dissolve sugar. Heat to boiling; boil 5 minutes.
Add cranberries; cook until skins pop (about 5 minutes). Remove from heat. Cool. Place in
refrigerator for two hours. Serve chilled in a cut glass serving bowl.

Prep/Cook: 15 minutes

Fresh Brussels Sprouts with Chestnuts and Thyme

Ingredients

1 pound fresh Brussels sprouts, washed and trimmed
1 cup chicken stock
¼ teaspoon salt
¼ cup butter
½ cup cooked sliced chestnuts
½ teaspoon thyme

Directions

Combine Brussels sprouts in saucepan with chicken stock and salt.
Bring to a boil. Reduce heat, cover, and cook until Brussels sprouts are crisp-tender. Drain.
Melt butter in small saucepan; add chestnuts and thyme. Cook over medium heat until butter
is browned. Stir to coat chestnuts. Pour over Brussels sprouts and toss lightly.

Prep/Cook Time: 20 minutes

Serves: 2

Blackberry Tarts with Devonshire Sauce

Ingredients

2 cups fresh whole blackberries
1 tablespoon sugar
4 prepared tart shells

Devonshire Sauce
¼ cup dairy sour cream
2 tablespoons soft-style cream cheese
1 teaspoon sugar

Directions

Wash and drain blackberries thoroughly, toss with the tablespoon of sugar, and set aside.

Devonshire Sauce
In a small mixing bowl stir together the sour cream, soft-style cream cheese, and sugar until smooth.

Spoon the blackberries into tart shells. Top with Devonshire Sauce. Enjoy!

Prep Time: 10 minutes

Serves: 2

Vienna

After the Opera: A Supper in Vienna

After the Opera: A Supper in Vienna

The Place- Vienna: City of music, art, powerful families— Land of Mozart, Hapsburg Princes, Lipizzaner stallions, and Freud.

Imagine a morning exploring the broad boulevards and narrow cobblestone streets of Vienna. Later you take an afternoon ride through the Vienna Woods and enjoy the beauty and peace. In the evening you attend an opera or a classical music performance at the Staapsoper—the elegant State Opera House. After the performance you go to a quaint café for supper with friends. Crystal, music, and candlelight surround you as you begin the evening.

Create your own evening in Vienna.

- **Read a history of the city.**

- **Review stories about famous citizens such as Freud.**

- **Purchase some classical music or opera music-Mozart, Beethoven, or Mahler.**

- **Rent a movie set in Austria such as <u>The Sound of Music.</u>**

- **Find a travel guide video to better picture the city, the interesting areas and magnificent buildings.**

Build up to the evening and, as the music plays, enjoy **A Wonderful Supper in Vienna!**

The Menu

- Toasted Ham Canapes

- Veal Vienna

- Buttered Noodles

- Lemon Almond Green Beans

- Vienna Woods Chocolate Delight

Wine

Pinot Noir

or

Chardonnay

Toasted Ham Canapes

Ingredients

1 cup chopped cooked ham
½ cup shredded Gruyere cheese
3 tablespoons mayonnaise
2 tablespoons melted butter
1 teaspoon horseradish
6 water biscuit crackers

Directions

Combine ham, cheese, mayonnaise, melted butter, and horseradish.
Spread on crackers.
Broil in oven until hot.

Prep/Cook Time: 10 minutes   Serves: 2

Veal Vienna

Ingredients

¾ pounds ground veal
¼ cup plain dry bread crumbs
1 egg
1 tablespoon dried onion flakes
½ teaspoon dried thyme
¼ teaspoon salt
¼ teaspoon pepper
4 tablespoons unsalted butter
1 cup beef broth
1 can (4 ounces) sliced mushrooms, drained
¾ cup sour cream
1 tablespoon Dijon mustard
¼ cup chopped parsley

Directions

In a large bowl, mix together the veal, breadcrumbs, egg, onion flakes, thyme, salt and pepper. Form into 12 meatballs, about 2 tablespoons each. In a large nonstick skillet melt 2 tablespoons of the butter, add meatballs, and cook for 3-4 minutes.
Remove the meatballs from the skillet to a shallow dish and set aside. Melt the remaining 2 tablespoons of butter in a large nonstick skillet. Add the flour and cook 1 minute. Whisk in broth and simmer 1 minute. Add meatballs and mushrooms. Cover and simmer 8 minutes, stirring halfway through cooking.
Over low heat, stir in the sour cream, mustard and parsley. Heat thoroughly. Serve the meat balls with warm, buttered noodles .

Prep/Cook Time: 30 minutes   Serves: 2

Buttered Noodles with Mushrooms

Ingredients

4 ounces noodles
¼ cup butter
6 medium-sized fresh mushrooms,
Wash, drain, and slice
Salt and pepper

Directions

Bring two quarts of water and one tablespoon of salt to a rapid boil. Add noodles. Boil uncovered, stirring occasionally, about 14-16 minutes or until noodles, are tender. Drain; rinse with hot water and drain again.
Saute mushrooms in melted butter. Stir in the noodles to blend. Add salt and pepper to taste. Serve warm.

Prep/Cook Time: 20 minutes   Serves: 2

Lemon-Almond Green Beans

Ingredients

8 ounces fresh green beans
1 green onion, thinly sliced (2 teaspoons)
1 tablespoon of butter
2 tablespoons slivered almonds
½ teaspoon finely shredded lemon peel

Directions

If using fresh green beans, cut crosswise into 1-inch pieces.
Cook, covered, in a small amount of boiling water till beans are crisp-tender. (Allow 20 to 25 minutes for 1-inch pieces.)

For sauce, in a small saucepan cook the green onion in hot butter until tender. Remove from heat. Stir in the almonds and lemon peel. Toss with hot drained beans.

Prep/Cook Time: 30 minutes   Serves: 2

Vienna Woods Chocolate Delight

Ingredients

½ cup butter
1 cup sugar
1 teaspoon vanilla
2 eggs
two 1-ounce squares unsweetened chocolate, melted
½ cup sifted all-purpose flour
½ cup chopped walnuts
½ cup white chocolate morsels
1 pint vanilla ice cream
½ cup raspberry sauce

Directions

Cream butter, sugar, and vanilla; beat in eggs. Blend in chocolate. Stir in flour, nuts, and morsels. Bake in greased 8x8x2 inch pan at 325 degrees for 30-35 minutes. Cool. Cut in 4 squares. Top with scoop of vanilla ice cream. Drizzle with raspberry sauce.

Prep/Cook Time: 45 minutes   Serves: 2

Rome

A Candlelight Dinner in a Roman Garden

A Candlelight Dinner in a Roman Garden

The Place – Rome: The Eternal City of Caesar, the Coliseum, the Baths of Caraculla, magnificent churches and fountains!

Just outside of Rome there are a number of beautiful villas and romantic gardens, flowers, and waterfalls. After a day of exploring ancient Rome in the morning and shopping on the Via Condotti (Rome's Fifth Avenue) in the afternoon, imagine you have been invited to an outdoor dinner in a Roman villa garden. The feeling of history surrounds you as you arrive. Create your own atmosphere of a Roman garden dinner with extra flowers, soft Italian music, and dine outside if you can - - with lots of candles!

As you build up to the evening -

- **Read a history of Rome.**

- **Purchase some magazines featuring Rome's sights and fashions.**

- **Rent a travel video on Rome.**

- **Watch some movies that feature sights of Rome such as <u>Roman Holiday,</u> <u>Three Coins in the Fountain</u>, or <u>Sparticus.</u>**

- **Purchase Italian music from opera to Dean Martin.**

Pick a warm spring evening, set a beautiful table outside, arrange the candles and flowers, and enjoy **A Candlelight Dinner in a Roman Garden!**

The Menu

- Antipasto

- Pasta Borghese

- Two Lettuce Salad
  in Oil and Balsamic Vinegar

- Italian Buttered Bread (purchased)

- Torta di Ricotta

- Cappuccino

Wine

Chianti

Antipasto

Ingredients

½ cup olive oil
1/3 cup wine vinegar
2 tablespoons water
1 clove garlic, cut in half
¼ teaspoon salt
Dash freshly ground pepper
one 9 ounce package frozen artichoke hearts, halved
1 medium head lettuce
2 hard-cooked eggs, sliced
Slices of Provolone and Gorgonzola cheese
Slices of Italian salami
6 pimiento stuffed olives, 6 ripe olives
1 tablespoon chopped chives

Directions

Combine oil, vinegar, water, garlic, and seasonings in small jar. Cover; shake well. Chill.
Cook artichokes according to package directions; cool and drain. Remove garlic from dressing. Pour over artichokes; chill 2 hours.
Line a platter with lettuce broken into bite-size pieces.
Add chilled artichokes, reserving marinade. Pour marinade over lettuce. Arrange eggs, cheeses, salami and olives around artichokes. Garnish with pimiento. Sprinkle with chives over all.
Serve with warm Italian bread and oil.

Prep/Cook Time: 2 ½ hours   Serves: 2

Pasta Borghese

Ingredients

½ box Angel Hair Pasta (8 ounce box)
12 fresh broccoli spears
2 cloves garlic
½ pound sweet butter
Fresh ground pepper
Salt to taste
1 tablespoon oil
1 cup Parmesan cheese

Directions

Cut broccoli into pieces about 2 inches long.
Cook broccoli in boiling water lightly-keeping it firm.
Melt butter in small saucepan.
Press garlic cloves into butter.
Cook pasta according to instructions on box.
Add oil. Drain pasta and return to pot.
Pour butter mix over pasta in pot.
Add broccoli and Parmesan cheese and mix thoroughly.
Add salt and pepper to taste.

Prep/Cook Time: 25 minutes   Serves: 2

Two Lettuce Salad
In Oil and Balsamic Vinegar

Ingredients

1 head Bibb lettuce
1 head red leaf lettuce
1 cup bread croutons
1 ripe tomato sliced into small pieces
½ cup olive oil
½ cup Balsamic vinegar

Directions

Wash and pull leaves from lettuces.
Break into bite-size pieces.
Arrange with tomato slices in small salad bowls.
Chill during cocktails.
Just before serving, sprinkle lightly with salt and pepper.
Add croutons.
Drizzle lightly with oil and balsamic vinegar.

Prep Time: 10 minutes   Serves: 2

Torta di Ricotta
(Cheesecake)

Ingredients

Crust
2 tablespoons superfine sugar
1 teaspoon grated lemon rind
1 cup plain (all-purpose) flour, sifted
¼ teaspoon vanilla
1 egg yolk
2 tablespoons, unsalted (sweet) butter, softened
2-3 tablespoons ice water

Filling
3 cups Ricotta cheese
1 cup superfine sugar
½ cup double (heavy) cream
3 tablespoons plain (all-purpose) flour
1 teaspoon vanilla
5 eggs, separated
raspberries or strawberries

Directions

Make the crust. Place the sugar, lemon rind and flour in a mixing bowl and mix well. Add the vanilla, egg yolk and butter. Beat until the mixture forms into a dough and the ingredients are well combined. Add ice water as needed to make dough come together to form a ball. Press half the dough mixture into a greased 9-inch spring form cake pan. Bake in a preheated oven at 400 degrees F for 8 minutes. Remove from oven, leave to cool, then press the remaining crust mixture onto the sides of the pan and set aside.

Make the filling. Place the Ricotta cheese in a bowl and beat until creamy. Mix in the sugar, cream, flour, vanilla, and egg yolks. Place the egg whites in a bowl and whisk until they are stiff. Gently fold the egg whites into the Ricotta cheese mixture. Pour the filling into the pastry-lined pan and bake in a preheated oven at 350 degrees F for 1 hour. Allow the cheesecake to cool in the pan. Chill. Remove from the pan and top with fruit before serving.

Prep/Cook Time: 25 minutes

Cappuccino

Ingredients

2 cups cold water
2 tablespoons sugar
¼ cup instant espresso coffee
½ cup whipping cream, whipped
Ground nutmeg

Directions

Bring water and sugar to boil.
Add coffee.
Stir to dissolve.
Pour into demitasse cups.
Top with whipped cream.
Sprinkle with nutmeg.

Prep Time: 15 minutes

Serves: 2

Greece

Swept Away – Alone on a Greek Island

Swept Away – Alone on a Greek Island

Place – Greece: Land of Homer, the Odyssey, and the Aegean and Ionian Seas with enchanting islands scattered among them.

Imagine a small Greek island – white stucco houses sparkling in the sunlight, deep blue waters, tiny villages with outdoor cafes, and restaurants with colored lights strung all around overhead to create a festive atmosphere. Envision a day of sailing among the islands. Later you find a waterfront café and sip a glass of ouzo as you watch the fishing boats return to port. As the sun sets the lights come on and you are ready for a Greek island dinner.

Create your own Greek island adventure.

- **Read the Illiad or the Odyssey.**

- **Purchase travel magazines that feature Greece.**

- **Watch videos showcasing the wonderful islands.**

- **Rent a movie about Greece such as <u>Zorba the Greek.</u>**

- **Wear a Greek island casual outfit.**

- **Consider dining on the deck, and string some colored lights around to create the atmosphere.**

Add your own ideas and get ready to be **Swept Away for a Greek Island Dinner!**

The Menu

- Ouzo over Ice

- Delphi Tray

- Greek Salad

- Mousaaka

- Santorini Rice

- Baklava

Wine

Apelia
A silky, dry Greek red wine

or

Merlot

Ouzo Begin your evening with a glass of Ouzo over Ice-the favorite of many who like to sit and observe the beautiful setting around them in Greece.

Delphi Tray

Ingredients

10 Greek olives in a serving dish
Pita bread (purchased)

Hummus
1/4 cup sesame seeds
1 can (15 ounce) garbanzo beans, drained,
(Reserve the liquid.)
4 tablespoons olive oil
3 tablespoons lemon juice
2 cloves garlic, chopped

Directions

In a small frying pan, toast sesame seeds over medium heat, shaking pan often, until golden (about 3 minutes). Transfer seeds to a blender or food processor and add garbanzos, 2 tablespoons of the oil, lemon juice, garlic, and 6 tablespoons of the reserved garbanzo liquid. Whirl, adding more liquid if needed, until hummus is smooth but still thick enough to hold its shape.
Season to taste with salt and pepper.
Transfer hummus to a shallow bowl.
Drizzle with remaining 2 tablespoons oil.
Spread hummus on pieces of pita bread and serve with olives.

Prep Time: 10 minutes

Greek Salad

Ingredients

1 clove garlic, cut in half
½ teaspoon salt
¼ teaspoon pepper
½ cup olive oil
½ cup wine vinegar
½ tablespoon lemon juice
1 small head lettuce, broken into bite-sized pieces
small wedge of red cabbage, shredded
1 green onion thinly sliced
1 tomato cut in eighths
½ pound feta cheese
6 ripe olives

Directions

Place garlic, salt, pepper, oil, wine vinegar, and juice of lemon in a small jar with tight fitting lid. Shake well. Toss ingredients together; add just enough dressing to coat greens. Crumble cheese and sprinkle over salad. Decorate top with olives.

Prep Time: 25 minutes   Serves: 2

Mousaaka

Ingredients

1 eggplant (about 1 pound)
1 tablespoon olive oil
1 teaspoon salt
½ pound lean ground beef
1 small onion, chopped
1 clove garlic, minced or pressed
4 small tomatoes
1 eight-ounce can of tomato sauce
1½ tablespoons of minced parsley
¾ teaspoon cumin seeds

Directions

Trim stem off eggplant. Cut eggplant into 1-inch cubes and mix with salt; drain in a strainer for about an hour. Rinse well under cool running water; drain and pat dry. Place oil in 10-inch frying pan over medium to high heat. When oil is hot, add eggplant; cook, stirring often, until cubes are lightly browned (about 6 minutes). Add 1½ tablespoons of water; stir eggplant, quickly cover pan, and continue to cook. About every minute, add another tablespoon of water, stirring eggplant and quickly covering pan, until eggplant is very soft. Add beef, onion, and garlic to pan; increase heat to high. Stir until meat is very well browned (about 8 minutes). Add juices, tomatoes, tomato sauce, cumin seeds, and parsley. Reduce heat, cover, and simmer until flavors blend and tomatoes are soft.

Prep/Cook Time: 1 hour   Serves: 2

Santorini Rice

Ingredients

½ cup wild rice
¾ cup chicken broth
1 cup chopped carrots
1 cup green peas
¼ teaspoon dried basil, crushed

Directions

Rinse rice with cold water in a strainer about one minute, lifting rice to rinse. In a one-quart casserole combine rice. In a small saucepan combine broth, carrots, peas, and basil. Bring to boiling; reduce heat and simmer, covered for about five minutes. Stir into rice mixture in casserole.
Cover and bake in a 350 degrees oven for 60-70 minutes or until rice is tender.

Prep/Cook Time: 1 hour 15 minutes

Serves: 2

Baklava

Flavors blend nicely if this recipe is made several days ahead.

Ingredients

4 cups walnuts (1 pound package) finely chopped
½ cup sugar, 2 teaspoons cinnamon, ½ teaspoon cloves
1 cup butter, melted; 1 cup honey, 2 tablespoons lemon juice, ½ cup water, ¼ cup sugar,
1 lb. phyllo dough (Phyllo is in the frozen-food section of most supermarkets.)

Directions

Grease a 13"x 9" baking dish. In a large bowl, combine chopped walnuts, sugar, ground cinnamon, and cloves with a spoon until blended; set mixture aside.
In baking dish, place one sheet of phyllo allowing it to extend up sides of dish; brush with some butter. Continue to layer sheets with butter until ½ of dough is used.
Spread the walnut mixture from bowl evenly over top of dough. Place another sheet of dough over the nut mixture, brush with butter, and continue layering phyllo sheets.
Cut into 2-by-2 inch squares. Bake for about 15 minutes until golden brown in a preheated 400 degrees oven. Cool.
Combine 1 cup honey, ¼ cup sugar, water, and lemon juice in a small saucepan; bring to a boil. Cook for a few minutes until the sugar dissolves and the mixture is well blended. Cool and pour over baklava.

Bavaria

An Evening on a Bavarian Mountaintop

An Evening on a Bavarian Mountaintop

The Place – German Bavaria: Land of snowcapped Alpine Mountains, beautiful castles, winding rivers, and mountain chateaus with flowered window boxes

Imagine a day exploring a charming Bavarian village with a late day visit to a beautiful castle where you observe the elegant rooms and dark dungeon. At dusk you take the incline ride to the top of a mountain and arrive at a cozy inn. You are shown to a table by the window with a view of the valley below and snow-capped mountains in the distance.

Create your own Bavarian Mountain Top evening.

- **Read a history of Germany and Bavaria.**

- **Look for picture books of Bavarian sights and castles.**

- **Rent a travel video on the region.**

- **Purchase some German music with an emphasis on classical and symphony artists.**

Wait for a cold autumn or winter evening and enjoy a fantasy trip to **A Bavarian Mountain Top!**

The Menu

- Alpine Cheese Spread

- Pumpernickel Bread

- Marinated Pork Roast

- Spaetzle

- Bavarian Squash

- Mountain Apple Dessert

Wine

Chardonnay

Pinot Noir

Alpine Cheese Spread

Ingredients

1cup small curd cottage cheese
1 small package (3 ounces) cream cheese at room temperature
2 teaspoons paprika
1 teaspoon *each* dry mustard and caraway seeds
salt and pepper
pumpernickel bread

Directions

Beat cottage cheese, cream cheese, paprika, mustard, and caraway seeds until smoothly blended.
Salt and pepper to taste.
If made ahead, cover and refrigerate for about two days.
Serve on pumpernickel bread.

Prep Time: 5 minutes

Marinated Pork Roast

Ingredients

2 cloves garlic, minced or pressed
½ cup olive oil
1 tablespoon grated lemon peel
½ cup lemon juice
½ teaspoon chopped fresh rosemary
1 teaspoon parsley
2 pounds pork loin
1 teaspoon each paprika and lemon pepper
4 slices of lemon

Directions

Make ahead: In a small bowl, combine garlic, oil, lemon peel, lemon juice, parsley, and chopped rosemary. Cover and refrigerate for at least two days.
Brush pork loin all over with lemon juice/garlic oil mixture, and place in two-quart rimmed baking dish with a cover. Let marinate for one hour or refrigerate for up to one day.
Sprinkle pork loin with paprika and lemon pepper. Wrap in tin foil folding foil across top, and place in a two-quart baking dish. Bake in 350 degree oven for about 50 minutes.
Unwrap tin foil and fold back from loin. Bake an additional 10-15 minutes until browned.

Prep Time: 10 min.   Cook time: 60 min.   Serves: 2

Spaetzle

Ingredients

½ bag (8.8 ounces) homemade spaetzle
2 cups clear beef stock
1 tablespoon finely chopped fresh parsley or chives

Directions

Bring 2 quarts water and 1 teaspoon salt to rapid boil. Add ½ bag of homemade spaetzle. Boil uncovered, stirring occasionally, about 14-16 minutes or until spaetzle is tender. Drain; rinse with hot water and drain again. Heat the clear beef stock and mix with the cooked spaetzle. Serve warm. Garnish with parsley or chives.

Prep/Cook Time: 25 minutes   Serves: 2

Bavarian Squash

Ingredients

1 acorn squash
2 tablespoons butter
2 tablespoons brown sugar
2 teaspoons nutmeg
Dash salt and pepper

Directions

Cut squash in half and scoop out seeds. Arrange, cut-side down, in a shallow baking pan. Surround with a small amount of hot water and bake in a 350 degrees oven for 30 minutes. Combine butter, brown sugar, and nutmeg in a bowl. Pour off liquid from baking pan and turn squash cut-side up. Spread glaze over squash. Bake 30 minutes, or until tender, basting now and then with sauce.

Prep/Cook Time: 70 minutes   Serves: 2

Mountain Apple Dessert

Ingredients

For filling
4 cups tart, peeled and sliced baking apples
1 ½ tablespoons lemon juice
1½ tablespoon flour
¾ cups sugar
1 teaspoon cinnamon
3 tablespoons butter (for filling)

For crust
½ cup flour
1teaspoon baking powder
¼ teaspoon salt
½ cup sugar
2 tablespoons of softened butter (for crust)
1 egg, beaten

Ice cream

Directions

Preheat the oven to 375 degrees F. For filling, place apples in a large mixing bowl and sprinkle with lemon juice. Stir in flour, sugar, and cinnamon, and place mixture into an 8 x 8 inch baking dish. Drop pieces of butter on top of mixture. In a separate bowl, sift together flour, baking powder, salt, and sugar. Add butter and egg. Mix together well. Drop batter by large spoonfuls on top of apple mixture. Spread evenly with a knife. Bake for 35-40 minutes. Serve warm with dollops of ice cream.

Prep/Cook 45 min.   Serves: 2

Russia

Moscow Nights: A Russian Dinner to Remember

Moscow Nights: A Russian Dinner to Remember

The Place – Russia: Land of strong traditions, czars, revolutions, icy winter landscapes, and romantic sleigh rides

Imagine you are in Moscow. You have spent a day visiting the sights of the city – magnificent buildings like Saint Basil's, the Kremlin, shops and busy streets. In the evening you go to the theater for ballet and on to an elegant restaurant where warm lights invite you in from the cold, snowy winter night outside.

Create your own dinner in Moscow. Learn about Russia as you plan the evening.

- **Read a history of Russia**

- **Enjoy some works of famous Russian writers –Tolstoy or Dosteovsky.**

- **Purchase music from the notable ballets and orchestras of Moscow.**

- **Rent a movie such as Dr. Zhivago.**

- **Find travel videos to help create the mood.**

- **Splurge and buy some caviar.**

Pick a cold January evening and enjoy **A Russian Dining Adventure!**

The Menu

- Iced Vodka

- Caviar on Toast

- Stuffed Cabbage

- Basil Roasted Potatoes

- Peas with Cheese

- Russian Winter Passion

Wine

Merlot

Caviar on Toast

(Prepare two glasses of Russian vodka over ice to help start the evening.)

Ingredients

There are many kinds of caviar. Visit a gourmet food store for a recommendation on the choices.

2 ounces of caviar (Purchased)
2 slices of toast
½ cup sour cream
¼ teaspoon minced onion
1 hard-cooked egg, diced
4 sprigs of fresh parsley

Directions

Blend sour cream, minced onion, and diced egg until smooth.
Place in small serving dish or bowl.
Serve caviar on top of sour cream mixture.
Place serving dish or bowl on round serving plate.

Cut slices of toast in quarters.
Alternate toast quarters with sprigs of parsley on the serving plate to surround the caviar/sour cream bowl.
Spread caviar/sour cream on toast quarters and enjoy!

Prep Time: 10 minutes

Serves: 2

Stuffed Cabbage

Ingredients

1 egg
1 teaspoon of salt, dash of pepper
1 teaspoon Worcestershire sauce
¼ cup finely chopped onion
1 clove garlic, minced
1 teaspoon crushed red pepper
½ cup milk
½ pound ground beef
½ pound ground pork
¾ cup cooked rice
6 large cabbage leaves
one 10 ¾ ounce can tomato sauce
1 tablespoon brown sugar
1 tablespoon lemon juice

Directions

In a bowl combine egg, salt, pepper, Worcestershire sauce, onion, garlic, red pepper, and milk; mix well. Add ground beef, ground pork, and cooked rice; beat together with fork. Immerse cabbage leaves in boiling water for three minutes or just until limp; drain. Place ½ cup meat mixture on each leaf; fold in sides and roll ends over meat. Place rolls in 12x7x2 inch baking dish. Blend together tomato sauce, brown sugar, and lemon juice; pour over cabbage rolls. Bake in 350 degree oven for 1¼ hours. Baste once or twice with sauce.

Prep/Cook Time: 1 hour 30 minutes   Serves: 2

Peas With Cheese

Ingredients

10 ounces of fresh garden peas
1 ½ tablespoons of butter
½ cup of cheddar cheese, small cubes

Directions

Thoroughly rinse and drain fresh peas. Place 1 cup of water in a saucepan. Bring water to a boil. Add peas. Cook over medium heat approximately 10 minutes or until tender. Drain. Toss hot peas with butter and cheese cubes.

Prep Time: 15 minutes   Serves: 2

Basil Roasted Potatoes

Ingredients

4 small red-skinned potatoes
½ cup green onions, chopped
1clove garlic, minced
½ cup olive oil
½ teaspoon basil
½ teaspoon paprika

Directions

Combine all ingredients in a small roasting pan
or dish. Prepare ahead of time and allow to baste for flavor.
Bake in 400 degree oven for 30 minutes.

Prep/Cook Time: 40 minutes   Serves: 2

Russian Winter Passion

Ingredients

4 scoops vanilla ice cream
½ cup chocolate syrup
1 cup fresh raspberries

Directions

Place two scoops of vanilla ice cream in dessert dishes. Drizzle chocolate syrup over ice cream. Top with fresh raspberries. Enjoy.

Serves: 2

Mexico

A Mexican Spa Evening

A Mexican Spa Evening

The Place – Mexico: Land of majestic mountains, captivating seaside resorts, and cultural sights.

Imagine a day walking on the beach, soaking in the sunshine, and exploring the sights and shops of a seaside village. You return to your hotel and decide to pamper yourselves at the spa.

Create your own Mexican spa evening. Build up to your evening by reading a history of Mexico and renting travel videos about the country. Most of all relax and escape to a wonderful Mexican Spa Evening!

- **Fill a tub with hot water and place lighted candles of all sizes about the room to give off soft romantic flames and dancing shadows.**

- **Make margaritas.**

- **Play some soft, sensuous Mexican music.**

- **Have a long luxurious soak together.**

- **Purchase some massage oil and give each other a vigorous massage-take a long time.**

- **Make love slowly.**

After your spa time, move on to **A Mexican Fiesta Dinner**—have another margarita! Dine outside if you can and add lanterns and streamers for a festive atmosphere.

The Menu

- Margaritas Curnevaca

- Chile Con Queso with Tortilla Chips

- Chicken Fajitas

- Rice Vera Cruz

- Acapulco Rum Pineapple Cake

- Carta Blanca Beer or Chardonnay Wine

Margarita Curnevaca

Ingredients

one 6 ounce can frozen limeade, thawed
8 ounces tequila
two ounces Triple Sec
six ounces water
juice from ½ lemon
ice
salt

Directions

Combine above ingredients in a blender. Add ice cubes to ¾ of blender. Blend thoroughly until ice is finely crushed. Serve in gimlet glasses. If desired, salt rims of glasses by dipping rims in lemon juice and rolling in salt.

Prep Time: 10 minutes   Makes 4 Margaritas

Chile Con Queso with Tortilla Chips

Ingredients

2 tablespoons salad oil
1 medium-size onion, finely chopped
1 can (4 ounces) diced green chiles
1/3 cup heavy cream
1 cup (4 ounces) shredded Longhorn Cheddar cheese
Crispy Tortilla Chips (Purchased)

Directions

Place oil in a 3- to 4-quart pan over medium heat. Add onion and cook, stirring, until soft (about seven minutes). Add chiles and cream; cook, stirring, until hot. Reduce heat and add cheese; stir until melted.
Pour into chafing dish over a low flame or into a dish on an electric warming tray set on low. Add salt and pepper to taste. Serve with crispy tortilla chips.

Prep/Cook Time: 30 minutes   Serves: 2

Chicken Fajitas

Ingredients

Two boneless, skinless chicken breasts
¼ cup water, 1tablespoon lime juice
½ teaspoon instant chicken bouillon granules
¼ teaspoon dried oregano, crushed
¼ teaspoon ground red pepper
four 10-inch flour tortillas, one teaspoon cooking oil
one clove garlic, minced; one chopped tomato
one avocado, halved, seeded, peeled, sliced
½ cup chopped celery
¼ cup plain yogurt, ¼ cup salsa

Directions

Slice chicken into bite-size strips. **For sauce-S**tir together the water, lime juice, bouillon granules, oregano, and ground red pepper in a bowl.
Wrap tortillas in foil. Heat foiled tortillas in a 350 degrees oven for 10 minutes to soften. Meanwhile, pour oil into a large skillet. Preheat oven to medium-high heat. Add the chicken and garlic to the hot skillet. Cook and stir for 2 to 3 minutes or to desired doneness. Add the sauce and tomato. Cook and stir for 3 to 4 minutes until tender and cooked thoroughly.
To serve, in the center of each warmed tortilla place chicken mixture, avocado slices, chopped celery, yogurt, and salsa. To fold the tortillas, bring up one edge of the tortilla to overlap the filling. Then, fold the two adjacent edges of the tortilla over the filling.

Prep/Cook Time: 55 minutes   Serves: 2

Rice Vera Cruz

Ingredients

1 ½ cups cooked rice
¼ cup sour cream
2 tablespoons chopped green chiles or green onions
½ cup grated cheddar or Monterey Jack cheese

Directions

Place half of the rice in a buttered dish. Combine sour cream, chiles and half the cheese in a mixing bowl. Spread over rice and cover with remaining rice. Sprinkle with cheese. Bake in a 350 degrees oven for 15 minutes.

Prep Time: 10 minutes

Serves: 2

Acapulco Rum Pineapple Cake

Ingredients

Cake Batter
½ cup sifted flour
½ cup granulated sugar
¼ teaspoon salt
½ teaspoon vanilla extract
¼ teaspoon baking soda
1 egg
¼ cup butter
¼ cup sour cream

Filling
2 tablespoons butter
1 (8oz.) can pineapple slices
¼ cup light brown sugar
1 small bottle maraschino cherries
1 tablespoon dark rum
1 (8 oz.) whipped cream topping

Directions

Preheat oven to 350 degrees F. Melt butter in a 9" x 5" loaf pan. Blend brown sugar, rum and salt into butter. Spread evenly over bottom of pan. Drain pineapple slices. Arrange 3 slices side by side in pan. Cut fourth slice into quarters; arrange pieces between slices along sides of pan. Place a maraschino cherry half, rounded side down, in the center of each pineapple slice. Cut remaining cherry halves in half again and arrange around outside of pineapple slices. Pour cake batter over fruit and distribute evenly. Bake 30 minutes until edges separate from pan and top springs back when lightly touced in center. Cool in pan 10 minutes. Loosen sides with a knife. Place a serving plate upside down over the pan and invert the cake onto a plate. Adjust fruit if necessary. Serve warm with Whipped Cream Topping.

Prep Time: 10 minutes   Serves: 2

Fantasy Romance

A Romantic Fantasy Evening at Home

A Romantic Fantasy Evening at Home

The Place: Anywhere You Want To Be

Imagine a castle, the woods, a penthouse, the beach –you can be anywhere you wish. Everyone has fantasies. It takes some courage and an adventurous spirit to suggest exploring them with your partner. Let your inhibitions go for an evening. Take turns exploring your desires by having an occasional fantasy evening.

Create you own version of a fantasy evening by building up to the evening all month long.

- **Pick a theme –Alone on a Deserted Island, Stranded on a Mountaintop or whatever excites you.**

- **Read some books and magazines to get ideas you can suggest to each other.**

- **Dress the part – whatever makes you feel romantic.**

- **Sip some champagne and sample courses as you share favorite fantasies.**

- **Let one person be in charge each time—be honest and open. Inspire each other!**

Relax, escape, open the champagne and enjoy **A Romantic Fantasy Evening at Home!**

The Menu

- Baked Brie with Apple Slices

- Honey-Buttered French Bread

- Oysters on the Half Shell

- Sweet Tomatoes

- Barbecued Beef Nibbles

- Butterscotch Squares

Wine

Champagne

Add to the adventure of the evening by selecting two champagnes and tasting as the evening develops!

Moet Chandon Brut Imperial

Veuve Cliquot

Pol Roget

Tattinger

Baked Brie with Apples
And
Honey Buttered French Bread

Ingredients

¼ pound Brie cheese cut in a wedge
1 teaspoon cinnamon
¼ cup sliced almonds
1 green apple washed and sliced

6 slices of French bread
½ cup butter
½ teaspoon honey

Directions

Whip honey into softened butter.
Spread on bread slices.
Bake in 350 degrees oven slightly to serve warm.

Place Brie wedge on heat-proof baking/serving dish.
Bake in preheated 350 degrees oven for 10 minutes.
Remove from oven.
Arrange apple slices and honey-buttered bread around Brie.

Prep/Cook Time: 15 minutes

Serves: 2

Oysters on the Half Shell

Ingredients

8 fresh oysters on the half shell
1 clove garlic, finely minced
½ cup butter
1 tablespoon dried parsley flakes
½ cup plain bread crumbs

Directions

Cook minced garlic and butter for 1 to 2 minutes. Toss lightly with breadcrumbs. Dredge oysters in mixture until coated. Place coated oysters in half shells on baking sheet. Sprinkle with parsley flakes.

Bake in 350 degrees oven for about 12 minutes.

Prep/Cook Time: 20 minutes   Serves: 2

Sweet Tomatoes

Ingredients

Two medium tomatoes
Two hard-boiled eggs, chopped
Three tablespoons mayonnaise
One sliced green onion
Dash curry powder
½ teaspoon soy sauce
1teaspoon lemon juice
1tablespoon parsley

Directions

In a bowl combine all ingredients except parsley.
Blend by tossing gently.
Fill tomatoes with mixture.
Garnish with parsley.

Prep Time: 10 minutes   Serves: 2

Barbequed Beef Nibbles

Ingredients

1 lb. sirloin or top round beef
2 ½ tablespoons soy sauce
2 tablespoons cold water
3 tablespoons sugar
1 tablespoon fresh minced garlic
¼ teaspoon black pepper
2 tablespoons toasted sesame seeds
1 tablespoon sherry cooking wine
2 stalks spring onions (cut into thin slices)
2 tablespoons sesame oil

Directions

Cut meat across the grain in very thin slices (this is easier if the meat is partially frozen).
Place in a glass or plastic bowl. Mix in water, sugar, soy sauce, garlic, pepper, sesame
seeds, and sherry with your hands till well blended. Press the meat down and cover.
Refrigerate for 4 to 8 hours (stir it three times while marinating).
Just before cooking, add spring onions and sesame oil and mix.
Cook over high heat for two minutes until browned on both sides in a frying pan.
Serve on a warm platter. Use toothpicks to pick up bite-sized pieces of beef.

Butterscotch Squares

Ingredients

½ cup softened butter
3 cups dark brown sugar
2 eggs beaten
1 teaspoon vanilla
6 cups of flour
2 teaspoons baking powder
½ teaspoon salt
1 cup chocolate bits
½ cup chopped nuts

Directions

Preheat over to 350 degrees.
Cream together softened butter, brown sugar, vanilla, and eggs.
In a separate bowl sift flour, baking powder, and salt. Add gradually to creamed mixture.
Stir in chocolate bits and nuts.

Pour mixture into lightly greased baking pan (9 x 13).
Bake at 350 Degrees for about 25 minutes. Let cool. Cut into 2" x2"squares.
Enjoy!

Prep/Cook Time: 35 minutes

Menus

Paris   **1**
Pernod over Ice
Stuffed Mushroom Caps
Chicken Veronique
French Green Beans
Rice St. Michele
Grand Marnier Crepes
Chardonnay

New York   **2**
Martinis -Vodka
Avocado w/Crabmeat
Madison Ave Salad
Lamb Fifth Avenue
Soho Asparagus
Potatoes Au Graten
Lemon Mousse
Merlot

Ireland   **3**
Irish Soda Bread
Salmon w/Mushroom Stuffing
Killarney Potatoes
Herbed Carrots
Wexford Pudding
Irish Coffee
Pinot Noir, Chardonnay

Shanghai   **4**
Sesame Shrimp Toast
Scallops w/ Ginger
Shanghai Vegetables
Steamed Rice
Lychee Paradise
Sauvignon Blanc

England   **5**
Shrimp Cocktail
Kensington Beef
Yorkshire Pudding
Brussels Sprouts
Kent Cranberry Chill
Blackberry Tarts
Cabernet Sauvignon

Vienna   **6**
Ham Canapes
Veal Vienna
Buttered Noodles
Lemon Almond Bean
Vienna Chocolate
Pinot Noir or
Chardonnay

Rome   7
Antipasto
Pasta Borghese
Italian Bread
Torta di Ricotta
Chianti

Greece   8
Greek Salad
Moussaka
Santorini Rice
Baklava
Apelia

Bavaria   9
Alpine Cheese Spread
Pumpernickel Bread
Marinated Pork Roast
Spaetzle
Bavarian Squash
Mountain Apple Dessert
Pinot Noir

Russia   10
Iced Vodka
Caviar on Toast
Stuffed Cabbage
Roasted Potatoes
Peas w/Cheese
Russian Passion
Merlot

Mexico   11
Margaritas Cunevaca
Chili Con Queso
ChickenFajitas
Vera Cruz Rice
Acapulco Rum Pineapple Cake
Chardonnay Wine
Carta Blanca Beer

Fantasy Evening   12
Baked Brie with Apples
Oysters on Half Shell
Sweet Tomatoes
Barbeque Beef Nibble
Butterscotch Squares
Champagne

www.ingramcontent.com/pod-product-compliance
Lightning Source LLC
LaVergne TN
LVHW061336060426
835511LV00014B/1943